Cheat

Kristin Butcher

ORCA BOOK PUBLISHERS

Library and Archives Canada Cataloguing in Publication

Butcher, Kristin
Cheat / written by Kristin Butcher.
(Orca currents)

Issued also in an electronic format.
ISBN 978-1-55469-275-0 (bound).--ISBN 978-1-55469-274-3 (pbk.)

I. Title. II. Series: Orca currents
PS8553.U6972C44 2010   JC813'.54   C2010-903579-8

First published in the United States, 2010
Library of Congress Control Number: 2010929086

Summary: Laurel investigates a cheating scam at her high school.

Mixed Sources
Cert no. SW-COC-001271
© 1996 FSC
FSC

Orca Book Publishers is dedicated to preserving the environment and has printed this book on paper certified by the Forest Stewardship Council.

Orca Book Publishers gratefully acknowledges the support for its publishing programs provided by the following agencies: the Government of Canada through the Canada Book Fund and the Canada Council for the Arts, and the Province of British Columbia through the BC Arts Council and the Book Publishing Tax Credit.

Cover design by Teresa Bubela
Cover photography by Getty Images

ORCA BOOK PUBLISHERS
PO Box 5626, Stn. B
Victoria, BC Canada
V8R 6S4

ORCA BOOK PUBLISHERS
PO Box 468
Custer, WA USA
98240-0468

www.orcabook.com
Printed and bound in Canada.

13 12 11 10 • 4 3 2 1

*For Britany, who gave gave
me the bones of the story.*

Chapter One

"*The homeless man claimed he had been sleeping in the school furnace room for over three months. 'The weekends were the best,' he said. 'There weren't no one in the school—not even janitors. I even took myself a shower in the boys' change room a time or two. Slept like a top those nights.'*"

Tara popped a grape into her mouth and continued reading.

1

"The man had used a ground-level vent to get into the building. Every night after dark, he removed the covering, lowered himself into the school basement and then pulled the vent back into place behind him. His hiding spot was discovered by accident. The vent cover fell off last week, attracting a curious skunk that decided to take a stroll through the school. When students and teachers started screaming and running for cover, the skunk took off back the way it had come. It was the custodian following behind who discovered the homeless man's makeshift bed behind the furnace. Police were called in, and the man was apprehended when he entered the building later that night. The skunk made a clean getaway."

Tara lowered the newspaper. "Well, good for the skunk. I feel bad for the guy though. He wasn't hurting anybody. He just wanted a place to sleep."

I waved my fingers at the newspaper. "Keep reading."

"*The school board hasn't pressed charges. In fact, school trustee Norma Swanson took the story to a city council meeting. She urged members to look into the matter. 'If there aren't sufficient shelters and soup kitchens to address the needs of this community's less fortunate, something needs to be done,' she told councilors.*"

"Let's hope Ms. Swanson's voice was heard." Tara put down the paper, ate another grape and looked at me wide-eyed. "Good story, Laurel!"

"You seem surprised," I said. I wasn't ready for *The New York Times*, but I was capable of stringing a few sentences together.

"I am."

My mouth dropped open.

"Well, not that you can write a good story," she backtracked. "It's just that this is way different from your usual stuff."

I sighed. "I know. Compared to reports on school dances and who's getting cosy with who, this story is definitely more meaningful."

"Exactly," Tara agreed. "It's important. It's news!"

"Right," I smiled. "Thanks, Tara."

"You're welcome, but—" She frowned. "Where did you get it? I mean how'd you find out about it? I knew about the skunk, but not the homeless guy."

I clucked my tongue and tried to look shocked. "Surely you don't expect me to reveal my sources?"

"Uh, yeah," said Tara. "I do."

I shrugged. "It was a combination of luck and eavesdropping. The day after the skunk incident, Miss Benson sent me to the office to get paper clips. The secretary wasn't there. While I was waiting for her to come back, I heard Mr. Wiens talking to some woman in his office. The door was wide-open, so the conversation was hard to miss."

"What were they talking about?"

"The homeless man. Mr. Wiens was telling the woman how he felt bad about kicking the guy out, because he had nowhere else to go."

"Who was the woman?" Tara asked.

"I'm getting there," I said. "Just listen. The woman said she would raise the issue at the next city council meeting."

Tara chewed on her lip.

"Ah…," she said. "I bet she's a trustee."

"Right." I nodded. "So anyway, after that I found out when the next city council meeting was, and I went. I had to sit for over an hour listening to half the city complain about streetlights and speed bumps before it was Ms. Swanson's turn. Talk about boring."

"Wow. You really did chase down this story. But how did you know about the guy showering in the boys' change room?" she asked. "Laurel Quinn, you didn't make that stuff up, did you?"

This time I was shocked for real. "Of course I didn't! After school I just hung around for a couple of hours. I thought maybe the guy would come back."

"And did he?"

I nodded. "He didn't try to get in, but he did come back. At first I wasn't sure it was him. But how many scruffy-looking guys stand outside a school for ten minutes staring at a vent? It had to be the squatter. So I went to talk to him."

"Weren't you scared?" Tara said. "I mean he could have attacked you or something."

"Ooh, I never even thought of that. Nothing happened though. The guy was actually pretty nice. He answered all my questions. All I had with me was five dollars, but I gave it to him. Hopefully he got something hot to eat. He sure needed it. He looked cold, and he was skinny as anything."

Tara straightened in her chair. "I guess you are a reporter. But isn't it going to kill to go back to writing about volleyball games and school debates?"

The bell rang, so I didn't have a chance to answer. I was definitely thinking about what Tara had said though. Reporting on normal school activities would be pretty tame now that I'd had a taste of real journalism.

Chapter Two

The paper had just come out at lunch, but it seemed like everyone had read my article by the time we went back to class. Walking to my locker was like strolling the red carpet. Every few steps, somebody would congratulate me—even kids I didn't know.

"Great story, Laurel."

"Super article."

"Good stuff."

I couldn't quit smiling. People had read my article and liked it. Even Jack complimented me on the story.

I thought I was seeing things. We might be brother and sister, but at school Jack barely acknowledges I exist. But there he was leaning on my locker door and grinning at me.

"Nice work, sis." He bopped my head with the rolled-up newspaper. "Good story. I liked the human-interest angle. Clever."

"Thanks," I said. Then, because it just wouldn't be normal if I didn't give him a hard time, I added, "Who knew you could read?"

He shot me a sour look. "Funny. Do you think half the colleges in the States would be recruiting me if I wasn't a brain?"

I rolled my eyes. "They don't care if you even *have* a brain, just as long as you can shoot a basketball. Let me guess—you saw the article Dean wrote about you." I snatched the newspaper from his hand and unrolled it. "Aha! I knew it." I smacked the page with the back of my hand. Then I read the headline. *Barton High Senior Destined for Greatness*. I clucked my tongue. "Don't believe everything you read, brother dearest. Dean tends to exaggerate."

"What are you talking about?" Jack frowned and grabbed the paper back. "Everything in here is true. I *am* being recruited by a half-dozen NCAA colleges. They've all offered me a free ride. Arizona, Oregon, Washington, Oklahoma—I just have to decide which one deserves me."

I rolled my eyes again. "Believe me—none of them deserves you. But by the time they realize it, it will be too late. You'll already be there."

"Was that a shot?"

"If you can't tell, I rest my case." I gave him a shove. "Now get out of here before someone sees us and figures out we're related. I don't want you wrecking my reputation."

He snorted and swaggered away.

Though he's a tough act to follow, I am proud of my brother. I would never tell him that to his face, but it's true. He is really smart. He gets almost straight As, and of course he's an amazing basketball player. Everybody likes him, including just about every girl in school.

So it is my duty to razz him whenever I can. Otherwise, he'd have such a swelled head, he'd have to find T-shirts with zippers.

At that moment, though, I was the one with the swelled head. I'd written an article that actually mattered, and people were reading it. That was pretty cool, considering the only reason I joined the newspaper was to do something Jack hadn't.

It's tough carving out a corner for yourself when you're related to a school legend. Almost anything I thought about trying, Jack had already done—in champion style. But now, after months of meaningless articles about nothing, I'd made a breakthrough. I was so pumped, my feet weren't touching the ground. I floated through the afternoon.

Mom's car wasn't in the driveway when I got home, but the front door was unlocked. That could mean only one thing—Jack had beat me home. I should say Jack *and Sean* had beat me home. Sean Leger doesn't actually live with us, but he and Jack have been best buds forever. If they're not playing basketball, they're sprawled in front of the television in our family room. I swear Sean spends more time at our house than he does at his own.

The two of them were all wrapped up in an air-hockey game, so they didn't see me come in. I could have walked off with the furniture, and they wouldn't have noticed.

"Where's Mom?" I shouted over their hooting and hollering.

"Drugstore," Jack yelled back as he made a shot. "He shoots, he scores!" He threw up his arms and did a victory dance.

Sean shook his head in disgust. "You got horseshoes up your butt, man."

Jack laughed as he flopped on the couch. "It's skills, pal. Skills. Eat your heart out."

Sean scratched his stomach. "Speaking of eating, whatcha got to chow on?" He headed for the fridge, messing my hair on the way by.

"Bug off," I said, giving him a hip check.

He grinned. "Is that any way for a big reporter to talk?"

"Yeah, right," I mumbled, trying not to smile.

"No, seriously. That was a good article," he said. "I liked it."

"Next stop, *The Globe and Mail*," Jack teased. "I almost forgot—there's a message for you. Not *The Globe and Mail*, but some guy from the *Islander*."

"Nice try," I retorted. I know my brother. There was no way I was going to let him suck me in.

"Really. I'm not kidding," Jack insisted, picking up the phone and punching in the message code. He held it out to me. "Listen for yourself."

I still didn't believe him, but I took the phone. I was all set to hear a dial tone, but there really was a message from someone at the *Islander*. The editor. He said his daughter was a Barton High student and had brought the paper home at lunch. He'd read my story and wanted to talk to me about it.

I quickly jotted down the phone number and took off to my room to return the call.

As I hung up the phone, I was numb. The *Islander* wanted to print my story about the squatter! It was going to run in Friday's paper. I was even going to get money for it. Just $25, but that still made me a paid reporter. Even better, the editor said he'd be interested in seeing future articles too.

I was so excited. I wanted to get writing that very second. The only problem was I had nothing to write about.

Chapter Three

By Monday morning, I was a celebrity. Everybody had seen the article in the *Islander*. Mr. Wiens even mentioned it during the morning announcements. It was embarrassing and thrilling at the same time. I didn't know how to look or what to say.

So I was actually grateful to have a math test after lunch. It took my mind off all the attention I was suddenly getting. I hadn't studied, so I should have been nervous. The way I look at it, though, you either know math or you don't. I was pretty sure I was okay with it.

My heart always speeds up before a test, but once I get started, I'm fine. I calm down and focus on what I'm doing. I just have to make it through those first few minutes of panic.

"Write your name on the answer sheet, and leave your test papers facedown until I tell you to begin," said Mrs. Abernathy as she handed out the tests. "You may use your calculators and scrap paper to work out your answers. In *pencil,* completely fill in the bubble of the correct answer for each question. Do not—I repeat—do *not* write on the test paper itself. Are there any questions?"

Her gaze swept the room. No one raised their hand. We all knew the drill.

"Good," Mrs. Abernathy said. "You will have the entire period to complete the test."

Which was getting shorter all the time. I glanced up at the clock. Just thirty-five minutes left.

"You may begin."

Twenty-five test papers flipped over. Right away I zipped to the last page. There were thirty questions, which meant just over a minute per question. Thank goodness the test was multiple guess. Teachers call it multiple choice, but let's be honest. For a lot of kids, it comes down to guessing. It seems to me tests would be more useful if students had to come up with answers from their brains. But that would mean teachers would actually have to mark them. With multiple-choice tests, they just scan the answer sheets, and the marking is done for them.

I have a system for tests. First I skim the whole thing to see what kind of questions there are. That helps me know how to use my time. Then I quickly do the questions I know I can answer. After all, a mark is a mark. Bottom line: get as many as you can. Some kids spend so long on one question that they don't finish. That's just plain dumb. I leave the hard questions for the end. And when in doubt—I guess.

There were about ten minutes left in the class. I was finished except for two problems. For some reason, my brain wasn't kicking in. I was doing grade-ten math, but at that moment it might as well have been rocket science. I looked up from my paper and stared into space, trying to make sense of the questions.

My eyes were open, but I wasn't really seeing anything—at least not at first. But then I became aware of something fluttering in the bottom left-hand corner of my field of vision. I zoomed in on it.

It was a hand—Dale Pearson's hand. He held it at seat level, up tight to his body. His thumb was tucked up and four fingers were extended. As I watched, he closed his hand into a fist and then opened it again. Now just one finger was showing. He held his hand like that for a few seconds before closing his fist again. When he opened it next, all five of his fingers were extended.

This clearly wasn't a case of writer's cramp. Dale was sending somebody a message.

I looked around. Two seats behind, Jarod Bailey had his eye on Dale's hand too. Every time Dale changed the position of his fingers, Jarod marked his answer sheet.

Ding! Ding! Ding! Bells started ringing in my head. Jarod was a solid D student. Dale got Bs. They were best friends. They were obviously cheating. There was no doubt in my mind.

It didn't take a genius to figure out the code they were using. A single finger told Jarod to fill in A, two was for B, and so on. Five fingers would be E.

I couldn't believe it. I knew kids cheated, but I'd never actually seen it before.

"One minute, people," Mrs. Abernathy announced in a robotic voice.

One minute! There was no time for me to finish the test now. All I could do was hope I was a good guesser. I wasn't too worried though. Two missed answers wasn't going to hurt me. I'd still pass.

Besides, the lost marks were worth it. Now I had a topic for my next article.

Chapter Four

The article on cheating almost wrote itself. That always happens when I'm fired up. My brain bubbles over, and the words spill out. I couldn't wait to see my story in print.

If kids were cheating in my math class, I had no doubt it was happening in other classes too. I'd stumbled on a real issue—one that a lot of kids probably didn't even know existed. If the editor at the *Islander* liked my last article, he was going to love this one.

I was at the dentist when the paper went on sale, and lunch hour was over when I got back to school. I snuck into the math room as quietly as I could and handed Mrs. Abernathy my late slip. Then I turned to take my seat and stopped. Everybody was glaring at me. They weren't just frowning because I'd disturbed them. They were totally telling me off with their eyes.

I wanted to run. It took all my willpower to walk to my desk and pretend everything was normal. I sat down, opened my books and made a big production of getting to work. It didn't help. I still felt every pair of eyes in the room—except maybe Mrs. Abernathy's—shooting death rays at me.

But why?

Jarod Bailey got up to sharpen his pencil. As he walked past, he dropped something on my desk and muttered, "Traitor."

I looked down. There was a copy of the school paper with a big black X through my story.

My mouth went dry, and my stomach did a flip. Apparently I'd gone from hero to villain.

"I don't get it," I complained to Tara and Liz as we walked home after school. "Everybody in my math class hates me! You should've seen the looks on their faces. Except for Jarod, not a single person spoke to me—*nobody*. And when the bell rang, the whole class took off like I had the plague."

Liz snorted and shifted the books she was carrying to the other arm. "What were you expecting? A ticker-tape parade?"

"What do you mean?"

Tara clucked her tongue. "Think about it, Laurel. You just ratted out your class."

"I did not!" I protested. "I didn't say who the cheaters were. I just wrote what they did."

Tara and Liz didn't look convinced.

"Okay, fine," I said. "I can understand why Jarod and Dale would be mad at me. They won't be able to cheat anymore. From now on, Mrs. Abernathy is going to be watching everybody like a hawk." My forehead buckled into a frown. "But why are the other kids mad?"

Tara rolled her eyes. "Because Mrs. Abernathy is going to be watching everybody like a hawk?"

"So?"

"So that means everyone is a suspect. Everyone except you, that is."

As Tara's words sank in, I said, "Oh. I never thought about it like that."

It was true. Not for a second had I considered that I was putting my classmates under a microscope.

Liz shifted her books again. "Why did you write that article, anyway?"

I blinked in disbelief. "You're kidding, right?"

Liz shook her head.

"Liz!" I said. "Kids were cheating!"

All she did was shrug.

I couldn't believe it. "Liz!" I exclaimed again.

"Oh, Laurel, take a pill," Tara said. "It's not like somebody robbed a bank."

"Yeah, it is," I argued. "Dishonesty is dishonesty. People who cheat on a test are the same kind of people who'd rob a bank."

"Oh, please," said Tara. "You've never copied an answer off someone else's paper?"

I shook my head. "No."

"Like I believe you," Tara snorted. "Everybody cheats."

I shook my head again. "Not everybody. I don't." I gestured toward Liz. "Liz doesn't."

I didn't know that for sure, but it was a pretty safe guess. Liz is the smartest kid I know. If teachers don't give her homework, she makes up her own. In all the years I've known her—and we go back to fifth grade—I have never seen her leave school without a stack of books.

I was shocked when she said, "Well, no, I've never copied someone else's answers—luckily, I've never had to. But I have let kids copy mine. Not very often," she said, "but when I know somebody needs a little help."

"That's not help!" I protested. "It's cheating!"

To my surprise, she grinned. "Oh, come on, Laurel. Lighten up. It's not a big deal. So somebody gets a couple

of extra marks on a test. So what? It isn't
going to stop the world from spinning. It
might save a kid from getting grounded
or cut from a team though."

"I can't believe what you're saying."

"Why?" asked Liz.

"Because you're smart. You're going
to be a doctor or a lawyer or the prime
minister or something. Why would you
help kids cheat?"

Liz just sighed. "Because it doesn't
matter. What happens at school only
matters at school. The real world doesn't
care."

I'd be lying if I said I wasn't surprised
by my friends' attitudes. I thought I was
doing a good deed by writing that article.
But nobody else saw it that way.

When I asked Jack what he thought,
he said I was overreacting too. Was I
the only person at Barton High who

knew the difference between right and wrong? Or were Liz and Tara and Jack right? Was I getting all bent out of shape over nothing?

I had to find out. And I knew just how to do it.

It took a bit of pleading to convince the editor of the school paper, but finally he agreed to let me run a survey on cheating in the next issue.

Monday morning I headed straight for the newspaper office. Through the window of the door I saw strips of paper strewn on the floor below the mail slot. *Yes!* Kids had filled out the survey. I let myself in. I didn't bother to move the survey slips to a table. I just flopped down on the floor in the middle of the mess.

I organized them into piles. The results were pretty discouraging. The box most often checked was *Not Concerned.* A few students selected *Slightly Concerned.* There were several *Unaware of Cheating* responses too. Only a couple of people checked off *Very Concerned.*

A lot of kids wrote comments. Most of them were less than friendly. *Get a life! Who cares? Don't be a troublemaker* were some of the kinder ones.

I sighed. This was not going the way I'd hoped. Then I saw it. It was a strip just like the others, except no box had been ticked. Instead, scrawled across it in red felt marker were the words *DRAPER'S SCANTRON TESTS. BIG-TIME SCAM.*

Chapter Five

I'd heard of Mr. Draper, but I didn't know anything about him. It's funny how that works. Unless teachers are standing in a classroom, you don't notice them. I'd probably passed the guy in the hall a hundred times, but I couldn't even tell you what he looked like. All I knew was that he taught grade-twelve math and biology. And the only reason I knew that much was because I asked around.

My informant had said a major cheating scam was going on in Draper's classes. Probably a lot of people were involved. The scam had something to do with the Scantron tests—those fill-in-the-bubble sheets. Scantron tests were marked by machine, so there had to be answer keys around somewhere. My guess was that someone had found them and made copies.

But I was only guessing. I had no evidence, and I couldn't write a news story based on an accusation scribbled on a scrap of paper. The *Islander* would never print it. I needed to prove the kids in Draper's classes were cheating.

Then *BAM!* It came to me. Their grades, of course. The cheaters should have better marks than the kids in the other classes.

It was a good theory, but once again I needed proof. Getting it was going to be a challenge. I couldn't go around asking kids to tell me their grades, and there was no way teachers would let me snoop through their mark books.

Wait a minute. What about the office? The marks of every single kid in the school had to be on computer. I couldn't walk in and print the marks off, but if I said I needed them for a story, I might be able to convince the principal to give them to me. But what kind of story would mean I had to look at student records?

I considered asking Jack's advice, but there was no point. He was too obsessed with choosing a basketball scholarship. He kept waffling back and forth, bouncing his arguments off anybody who'd listen. All he could talk about was which university he should choose.

Wait a minute, that was it—university. I would say I was writing an article about the connection between grades and university placement.

I decided to run my idea past Tara.

"Forget this scam," she said. "I bet you anything it's a hoax. Some kid probably made it up to send you on a wild-goose chase. I say go with the university placement thing. It would make a good article—if you can get the office to give you the records." It sounded like Tara didn't think I could.

"Mr. Wiens isn't going to give me records with kids' names—I know that," I conceded, "but he might give me a breakdown of marks by subject."

"What good will that do?" Tara asked. "If you don't know who the marks belong to, how are you going to figure out who their teachers are?"

I waved away Tara's objection. "I'll make up a reason to get class lists too."

She frowned. "How is that going to help?"

"Easy." I grinned. "The student records will be in alphabetical order. I'll simply combine the class lists into one huge list also in alphabetical order. Then I'll match the two up and bingo! I'll know who is getting what mark, and I'll know what class they're in."

Tara opened her mouth to say something, but all that came out was a squeak. I wasn't sure if she was impressed with my brilliance or shocked by my sneakiness.

Even though I'd had all the answers for Tara, I knew Mr. Wiens would be harder to convince. But it was worth a try, so on Tuesday I made an appointment to meet with him after school. I spent the last period, English class, planning what I was going to say.

I was only in Mr. Weins's office five minutes, but it felt like an hour. I'm not very good at lying—lack of practice, I guess—so I was really nervous. A hot river of perspiration started running down my back the second I sat down. By the time I stood up again, my T-shirt was pasted to my back.

Mr. Wiens didn't say much. Mostly he just leaned back in his chair, made a tent of his fingers and nodded. So I just kept talking. When it was over, I couldn't remember a thing I'd said.

I must have made a few good points though, because the next afternoon he called me back to his office and handed over everything I'd asked for.

"Barton students have an impressive history," he said, placing the papers inside a file folder. "Statistics indicate that about thirty-three percent of Canadian high school graduates continue on to university. Barton High is well above the national average. Last year thirty-nine percent of our graduates were university-bound. I expect that number to be even higher this year."

He pulled one of the papers from the folder and showed it to me. "You didn't ask for this, but I thought it might be helpful," he said. "This is a comparison of last year's grade-twelve marks and this year's. As you can see, math and biology averages are significantly improved."

That made sense. If kids were cheating in those subjects, averages would go up. Of course, I didn't say that to Mr. Wiens. I just nodded and mumbled, "That's very interesting."

He stuck the paper back in the folder and handed it to me. "I hope this helps you with your story, Laurel. I look forward to reading it."

Inside, I cringed. Why did he have to say that? Now I felt like I really had to write the article.

I forced a smile. "Thanks, Mr. Wiens. I'm sure this information is going to be a big help."

It was the truth, in a roundabout way. It *might* help me get to the bottom of the scam. I felt a little guilty about misleading Mr. Wiens though. But being a reporter meant digging, and that could be dirty. If it meant uncovering the truth, it was worth it.

As I left the office, I spotted Jack slouched against a wall of lockers. He was talking with Sean. I could only see Sean's back, but I had no doubt who it was. I'd recognize his back anywhere.

I started toward the two of them but had only taken a few steps when Jack banged his fist on the locker and growled, "Forget it!"

I stopped walking.

"No." He pushed himself away from the lockers and got right into Sean's face. "Not again."

He was obviously angry, and from the way Sean kept clenching and unclenching his fists, I could tell he was too.

What was going on? Jack and Sean never argued. I held my breath. Then suddenly Jack shrugged, and the tension seemed to leave his body. He said something I didn't hear, and Sean looked over his shoulder in my direction.

Sean faked a smile and waved. "Hey, Laurel," he said. Then he turned and jogged off down the hall.

I walked over to Jack. "What was all that about? You guys looked like you were getting ready to punch each other's lights out."

Jack shrugged. "Don't exaggerate. We were just having a difference of opinion about a play Sean wants to run. It's no big deal. See you at home."

Then Jack took off too.

Chapter Six

My original plan was to study the information Mr. Wiens had given me in the privacy of my bedroom. But once the file folder was in my hands, I couldn't wait. I needed answers right away.

The school had pretty much cleared out. I slipped into an empty classroom and spread the papers on top of a couple of desks. There were about two hundred grade-twelve students at our school. It would take forever to make a master list, so I settled for a mini-list of math students whose names started with *A*, *B*, and *C*. I hoped it would be enough to tell if there was a pattern to the marks.

Mr. Draper taught the only grade-twelve biology classes, so I didn't have to bother combining lists for that subject. If my informant was correct, kids in those classes were cheating. Not a single student was failing biology. That confirmed that at least some of them were cheating.

I was still surprised by the marks. I had expected them to be higher. There were a few As and Bs, but there were also a bunch of Cs and even a couple of Ds. If kids were cheating, the marks should have been better.

Unless the cheating scam hadn't been going on very long.

Of course! That had to be it. Students had probably only messed with one or two tests. It would take more than a couple of tests to bring course marks up a couple of letter grades.

I decided to check out Mr. Draper's classroom. I had no idea what it was going to tell me—maybe nothing. It didn't really matter. I needed to get a feel for the scene of the crime.

Mr. Draper taught math in room 132, which was connected to the biology lab by a small office. When I got there, the door was closed. I peered through the window. The classroom was empty. I knocked. Nothing. I grabbed the doorknob and turned, fully expecting it to resist. But the room wasn't locked.

"Mr. Draper?" I called as I pushed open the door.

My words hit the walls and slid to the floor. Mr. Draper wasn't there. This was good, because if he'd answered me, I would have peed my pants. I took a deep breath, peered up and down the hall and tiptoed into the room.

It was just another grungy, end-of-the-day classroom. There were scraps of paper on desktops and crumpled paper balls on the floor. Beneath my runners, I felt the accumulated grit of eight periods of kids tracking in dirt. The whiteboard was filled with math equations in red, blue and green marker.

Mr. Draper's desk at the front of the room was heaped with textbooks and binders. There was one dinky little corner where a coffee-stained mug and a tin can of pencils clung to the edge. I wondered how many times Mr. Draper had gone for a gulp of coffee and ended up with a mouthful of pencils.

Across from me was a wall of windows with the blinds pulled down—probably to keep kids from looking outside. Teachers are always shutting out the day. It makes you wonder why they bother putting windows in classrooms in the first place. Between the windows and Mr. Draper's desk was a filing cabinet.

I tiptoed past the desk to check out the glass-walled office. Cupping my hands around my eyes to cut out the glare, I squinted through the glass. The only furniture was a chair, another filing cabinet and another desk mounded with books and papers. On the far wall, a second door opened into the biology lab.

I tried the doorknob. This door *was* locked. Was the answer key in there?

I wandered around the classroom. There wasn't a lot to see except a notice on the corner of the whiteboard announcing an upcoming test. Another opportunity for the cheating scam to kick in? I made a mental note of the date.

Even though I was skulking in a strange classroom uninvited, I couldn't bring myself to snoop through Mr. Draper's desk. When I'd learned as

much as I could from walking around—
which was almost nothing—I decided
to leave. As I headed back to the door,
I heard footsteps in the hall. They were
close—*and getting closer*—

I looked for a hiding place. I didn't
want to have to explain to anyone what
I was doing there—not even the custodian.
Whoever was out in the corridor might
walk right on by, but I didn't want to take
the chance.

The only cover was the filing cabinet.
I squeezed in between it and the wall of
windows. I had to scrunch down so that
my head didn't show.

Right away, I regretted my choice. I'm
not good in small spaces. Being wedged
into a crevice barely big enough to hold a
flip chart—which was already there—felt
more than a little cramped. My arms and
legs were going in different directions.
I felt like one of those distorted figures
in an ancient Egyptian painting.

Then, suddenly, I wasn't alone. I heard the soft padding of feet followed by the scraping of wood on wood. There was a jangling noise and then more footsteps.

Was it Mr. Draper? I wished I could see. I needed to move, but I didn't dare. My legs were aching with the strain of crouching. My arms felt like they'd been shoved into their sockets backward. The more I thought about how uncomfortable I was, the worse I felt. If I didn't distract myself, I was going to go nuts. I pictured myself jumping out of my hiding spot like a jack-in-the-box.

I shut my eyes to make the image go away. I forced myself to focus on the sounds. I heard the jingling noise again. *Keys!* Whoever was in the room unlocked the door to the little office. The keys must have been in the desk—that was the wood-on-wood scraping I heard. Then there was a metallic rolling sound.

It was probably the filing cabinet in the little office being opened.

I was getting desperate to straighten my legs when the filing cabinet drawer rolled shut with a bang.

I froze. My legs were shaking. They weren't going to hold out much longer.

The office door banged shut, and the keys clinked in the lock. Then they landed with a crash back in the desk drawer. *Slam!*

In the silence that followed, I strained my ears to the limit. Did I hear footsteps walking away? Or was that only what I wanted to hear?

I tried to be patient, but I was dying. My legs were killing me! I could not stay crouched another second. In one motion I stepped out of the crevice and straightened up. The ache in my legs drained out through my feet. Suddenly the bigger issue became, *Was the person gone?* That's when I realized my eyes were still squeezed shut.

I opened them a crack and peeked through my eyelashes. I was alone in the classroom. I was safe, but I was also majorly curious. I wanted to know who'd just left. I hurried to the door and poked my head into the hall.

It was empty except for a boy walking away. I clapped a hand over my mouth to stifle a gasp and ducked back into the classroom.

I'd recognize that back anywhere.

Chapter Seven

I sagged against the wall. My legs were too exhausted to take any more stress—my knees gave out. I slid to the floor. For a couple of minutes I just sat there, staring at the closed blinds.

I couldn't believe it. Sean Leger had been in Mr. Draper's classroom. Sean, my brother's best friend.

Don't jump to conclusions, I told myself.

Okay, maybe it *wasn't* Sean. After all, I'd only seen the guy's back. Maybe it was somebody else. A lot of guys probably looked like Sean from behind.

And walked like him? And wore the exact same clothes? That was too much of a coincidence. Sean was definitely the person I'd seen in the hallway.

So what if he was? Just because Sean was in Mr. Draper's classroom didn't mean he'd done anything wrong.

I tried to come up with a reason—*any reason*—for Sean to be rooting around in that filing cabinet. I couldn't think of a single thing. He'd pulled the keys from the first drawer he opened, so he obviously knew where they were kept. Maybe he'd taken them before.

The only explanation was that he'd been searching for the answer sheet to the next math test. From the way he'd slammed the filing cabinet drawer, I was betting he hadn't found it. I glanced up at the notice on the whiteboard. The test was next week.

I didn't want Sean to be guilty. I'd known him my whole life. But what other explanation was there?

Just when I was sure my brain had gone on strike, the answer smacked me in the face. It was so simple. If Sean wasn't in Mr. Draper's classes, he wouldn't have any reason to steal the answer key. That would prove he was innocent.

I looked down at the folder I was still clutching. One side was totally crumpled. It didn't even go back into shape when I loosened my grip. The papers inside were crinkled too. I shuffled through them, searching for the lists of math classes.

Which one was Sean in? Barsky's? Timmons's? Walters's? Draper's? I skimmed each list. No, no, no…yes.

Rats!

I tried to stay optimistic. So Draper was Sean's math teacher. It didn't prove anything.

So why didn't I believe that?

Wait a second. The scam was going on in biology too. I riffled through the papers again. Sean and Jack were best buds. Jack took chemistry. Maybe Sean did too. I scanned the chemistry lists. I found Jack, but not Sean.

Okay, Sean wasn't in chemistry. Maybe he was a physics student. I checked the physics list—no Sean Leger.

All grade twelves had to take a science. If Sean wasn't in chemistry or physics, there was only one other alternative. I flipped through the biology class list. Bingo.

When I poked my nose into Jack's bedroom that evening, he had college stuff spread out everywhere. There were forms and brochures—on his desk, on the bed, even on the floor. Finding a place to stand was like playing Twister.

"Haven't you picked a school *yet*?" I asked as I straddled a calendar from Oklahoma State and a brochure from Gonzaga. "That's a new one, isn't it?" I said.

Jack frowned. "Mmm-hmm. He tapped another brochure. "So is this Stanford one. That's why I haven't made a decision yet." He looked up and shook his head. "This isn't easy, you know."

I scanned the mass of booklets and papers. "I guess not," I replied. "Have you read all this stuff?"

"Only about fifty times," he muttered.

"So what's the problem?"

Too late, I realized my mistake. Jack started in on the trials of choosing a college. "All of these schools have great basketball teams. I know I'll ride the pine the first year no matter where I go, but I'll also get some fantastic coaching. I'll have to make the most of the court time I do get. Of course, my big dream is to get drafted into the NBA. But I can't count on that. So I want a college with a good academic program. If basketball doesn't pan out, I'm going to need a career."

"In what?"

Jack threw up his hands. "That's the thing. I don't know! I'm thinking law, but part of me wants to be an architect, and another part is interested in business."

"Wouldn't the courses be really different for all those professions?"

"Exactly," he groaned. "And each college has its own academic strengths." He tossed a brochure over his shoulder. It landed on the bed. "I have no clue what to do. The more offers I get, the harder it is to decide."

"What do Mom and Dad say?"

Jack rolled his eyes and snorted. "Dad says to pick the college with the most options, and Mom says follow my heart."

"Hmm," I mumbled.

Jack looked at me hard. "What do *you* think I should do?"

"Whoa," I said, putting up my hands. I took a step backward—right onto a pile of forms from Washington State. "Oops, sorry," I apologized. "I can't make that decision for you. I have enough trouble deciding what clothes to put on in the morning."

Jack scowled. "Well, if you didn't come here to help me, what do you want?"

"Well," I drawled, "I was kind of hoping you could give *me* some advice."

"About what?"

I had no idea how Jack would react to what I had to say, but there was only one way to find out. I took a deep breath and plunged in. "Remember how I ran that survey in the school paper about cheating?"

"Yeah. What about it?"

"Well, I got a note back about a big cheating scam in Mr. Draper's classes. Something to do with the Scantron tests."

Jack let loose a huge laugh. "And you believe that?"

I felt my back stiffen. "I'm a reporter, Jack. It was a lead. So I followed it."

He stopped smiling. "Okay. So what did you find? Nothing, right?"

"Wrong." I told him how the marks and class lists supported the whole scam thing. "So I went to Mr. Draper's classroom to look around."

"And?"

I shrugged. "There was a notice on the board about an upcoming test."

"Ooh, good work, Sherlock," he snickered.

"I'm not finished," I told him coldly.

"Oh, sorry," he said, but I knew he wasn't.

I told him about someone ransacking the filing cabinet in Mr. Draper's office. I told him how I peeked into the hall just as the person was getting away.

"It was Sean," I said.

Jack looked like he didn't believe me.

"It was Sean," I repeated.

To my surprise, he just made a face and retorted, "So?"

"What do you mean, *so*? Don't you think that's incriminating?"

"No."

"How can you say that? The guy took a key from the desk and broke into the office. He was rifling through the filing cabinet."

Jack crossed his arms over his chest. "You're so caught up in this espionage fantasy that your brain has gone on vacation. Did you ever stop to consider that maybe Sean was *supposed* to be there? Sean is Draper's lab assistant. Did you know that?"

Now I felt stupid. "Oh. Uh, no. I didn't."

"Well, he is. Of course he knows where Draper keeps his keys. He's always having to get stuff for him."

"Oh," I said again.

"Forget this cheating thing," Jack grumbled.

"It's a news story, Jack," I argued. "And news isn't always pretty."

"There are a billion other things you could write about. I'm telling you, Laurel—everybody's talking. And what they're saying isn't good. Nobody likes a snitch. Unless you're looking to become a total outcast, let it go."

Chapter Eight

I wanted to believe what Jack had said about Sean, but part of me wasn't convinced. Sean was Jack's friend. Of course he was going to defend the guy. Don't get me wrong, I liked Sean too. But that didn't mean it was okay for him to cheat. Since I couldn't prove anything— at least not yet—I decided to keep my suspicions to myself.

"How goes the Scantron article?" Liz asked at lunch the next day.

I glanced around the lunchroom. "Not so loud. Somebody might hear."

Tara shook her head. "Honestly, Laurel," she said. "Do you really think anybody besides you cares?"

I felt myself bristle, but I didn't want to get into another argument. I let Tara's insult fly on by. As casually as I could, I said, "Mr. Wiens gave me the class lists and student marks." I was hauling food out of my lunch bag as I spoke, but I still saw Tara's jaw drop.

"He didn't!" She couldn't hide her amazement.

"Yeah, he did." I tried not to gloat.

"And?" Liz said.

"And it looks like my informant was right."

Tara gasped. "You mean there really *is* a cheating scam?"

I nodded.

"How can you be sure?" asked Liz.

"Well, for one thing, every single kid is passing biology. And the same goes for Mr. Draper's math classes. There are no failures there either."

"What about the other math classes?" Liz asked.

"At least a couple of failures in each one."

"Hmm. Very interesting," Liz said. "You'd think the administration would pick up on that."

"Maybe Mr. Draper is just a really good teacher," Tara argued. She clearly didn't want there to be a scam.

"Maybe," I conceded, "except that last year there *were* failures in Draper's classes."

"Really?" Liz asked. I could almost see the wheels in her brain starting to turn.

"How do you know that?" Tara demanded.

I took a bite of my sandwich before answering. "Mr. Wiens gave me last year's student marks too. So I could compare. He made a point of telling me that this year's grade twelves are doing better than last year's."

"Are all the kids in Draper's classes getting As?" Tara said.

I felt my forehead buckling. "No. They're not. That's the part I don't understand. Everybody's passing, but there's still a normal spread of marks—As, Bs, Cs and Ds. There's a little of everything, except Fs."

"Well, there you go." Tara announced smugly. "If there was a scam, *everyone* would be getting As."

Liz shook her head. "I disagree."

"Why?" Tara was instantly defensive.

"Maybe the person behind this operation is very clever. Think about it. If all—or most—of the kids in

Mr. Draper's classes started getting As, he'd know something was up. I don't care if he's the best teacher in the universe, some kids just don't get the concepts. *I* think students are getting custom cheat sheets. That way everybody passes, but nobody gets a perfect score. The marks are decent but still believable." She smiled again and nodded smugly. "Yes, very clever."

"I like your theory," I said, "but how do we prove it?" I was relieved that someone besides me finally believed a scam was going on.

Liz took a deep breath. "I have an idea."

"Shoot," I said.

"For starters, not all the kids in Draper's classes are in on the scam."

"You don't know that," Tara snapped.

Liz rolled her eyes. "When is there ever one hundred percent participation in anything? Some kids might be too honest to cheat." Liz glanced meaningfully in my direction. "Or—more likely—they just don't need to. Why would an A student bother cheating?"

Even Tara couldn't argue with that logic.

"But," Liz continued, "whether they're participating or not, they're going to know about it. All we have to do is convince one of them to tell us what they know."

I rubbed my hands together. "Sounds like a plan."

"Maybe—if you know who to talk to. Which you don't." Tara said.

"I have the class lists," I reminded her. "I'll get all the A students' names tonight. Someone is bound to talk."

Liz crumpled her muffin wrapper and wiped her hands on her jeans. "No need," she said. "I know exactly who to talk to."

"Who?" Tara and I said at the same time.

Liz grinned. "Draper's star student. My sister."

I was lying across my bed doing homework when Liz called that evening. I was in the middle of a history assignment, and I hate history. Her call couldn't have come at a better time.

I grabbed my cell phone and rolled onto my back. "Hello."

Liz got right to the point. "I talked to Hannah," she said.

"And? What did she say?"

"Not much," Liz said. "At first she would only admit to knowing there was a scam. My sister might be a brain, but she has no desire to commit social suicide." Liz made a production of clearing her throat.

I got her drift, but I ignored it.

"You said, 'At first.' Does that mean she eventually told you more?"

"Yes. But only after I blackmailed her. Even then I had to swear on my life nobody would ever know that she blabbed."

"What did you blackmail her with?"

Liz clucked her tongue. "I may need to play that card again. It wouldn't be much of a threat if Hannah's secret was already out there, now would it?"

I sighed. "No. I suppose not." I pushed Hannah out of my mind and cruised back on track. "So what's the scoop?"

"Well"—Liz dragged out the word—"I was right about this being a clever operation. And you were right about the crook making a copy of the answer key. But get this." She snickered. "The scammer *sells* the answers to the other kids in the class."

"*Sells* them?"

"Mm-hmm." I could almost hear the smile in Liz's voice. "How's that for an unexpected twist?"

I was momentarily stunned. I hadn't considered that money might be involved. It looked like the Scantron scam wasn't just a matter of cheating to pass a test. It was a business!

"Who's doing this?" I asked.

"I don't know," Liz said. "Hannah wouldn't name names. But, if she told us everything, you wouldn't have to do any digging at all. What fun would that be?"

"What else did Hannah say?" I wanted all the details.

"Whoever is doing this is in it for the long haul. The guy—Hannah did slip and say *he* a couple of times—sells each kid a different answer key based on the marks they usually get. So a C student gets a C answer key—or maybe a C+. But it's always in the normal range. The higher the grade, the more expensive the cheat sheet. Hannah says they range from seven to twenty dollars."

"You're kidding!" I squeaked. "How many customers does this guy have?"

"According to Hannah, about ninety percent of the kids buy in. Draper has two biology classes and two math classes. That's about a hundred and twenty kids. If ninety percent of them take part, that's a hundred and eight kids. Let's say one week there's a math *and* biology test. If the guy averages twelve dollars a sale, he would make"—there was a pause as she worked the calculation in her head—"about thirteen hundred dollars."

"Wow," I breathed. "That's a lot of money. By the way, do you know you sound like a math problem?"

Liz chuckled.

"Did your sister say anything else?" I ask.

"Yeah. Apparently our genius lives close to the school. The sales take place at his house during lunch."

"So how do the kids hand in their cheat sheets? Does our scammer make the switch?"

"No. The only risk he takes is copying the original answer key. The kids have to figure out how to switch the sheets on their own. Most of them smuggle them into the test under their shirts and make the switch sometime near the end of the class when Draper isn't looking."

"And nobody's been caught?"

"Not a single person."

"And nobody's squealed?"

"Not yet."

"Well, it's time somebody did."

I rolled onto my stomach again and saw Jack standing in the doorway. He'd obviously been listening.

He sent me a look that was a combination of pity and disgust, shook his head and walked away.

Chapter Nine

Liz had said the guy behind the scam lived close to the school. Sean lived close to the school. That was one more strike against him. I was sure he hadn't snagged the answer key when I'd seen him in Draper's classroom, but he could've gotten it since. With the test date creeping up, he might be in selling mode. It was time to keep an eye on him.

I decided to tail him at lunch on Friday. I tore off toward his locker as soon as the bell rang. As I waited for him to show up, I tried to get lost in the mob of kids dumping off books and grabbing lunches.

It wasn't long before Sean showed. He crammed his books into his locker and took off. I followed him to the exit and watched as he jogged across the field toward his house. All I had to do was wait. Once he was out of sight, I'd follow. There were bushes near his house where I could hide and spy on anyone who paid him a visit.

As I went to push open the door, a hand gripped my arm.

It was Jack.

"What do you think you're doing?" he sneered.

"It's none of your business," I snapped. "And let go of me." I yanked my arm free.

"You're following Sean," he said. "I've been watching you." He didn't look amused. "You're a crappy detective, Laurel. The only one getting caught is you."

I glared at him and reached for the door again, but again he grabbed my arm. This time it hurt.

"I mean it, Laurel," he said through gritted teeth. "Back off. Sean is my friend. I'm not going to let you drag him through the mud just so you can get a stupid newspaper story."

I opened my mouth to argue, but he cut me off.

"All you're doing is looking for glory. You don't give a rip about the people you're hurting."

"So you admit Sean's guilty," I sneered.

It was like Jack was a blow-up doll, and I'd just stuck him with a pin. His shoulders sagged, and his head drooped.

"You don't get it, do you? I'm asking you to leave this alone." Then he let go of my arm and walked away.

All afternoon I thought about what Jack had said. Part of me wanted to do what he asked. But the reporter in me couldn't let it go. If Sean was guilty, he'd done it to himself. If he wasn't guilty, great. Either way, there was a story here, and it needed to be told.

After school I decided to make another visit to Mr. Draper's classroom. If Sean—or whoever the Scantron Scammer was—didn't have the answer key yet, he might try again today.

This time the classroom wasn't empty. Mr. Draper was there. At least, I assumed it was Mr. Draper. When I peeked through the window of the door, I saw a dumpy bald guy with glasses sitting behind the desk. He didn't spot me, but seeing him there almost gave me a heart attack! I spun away and waited for the blood to stop pounding in my ears.

I peeked through the window again. If Mr. Draper was making up the answer key, the crook couldn't have stolen it yet. At first I couldn't tell what Draper was working on. But when he dropped his pencil and bent over to pick it up, I saw the Scantron sheet on his desk.

I felt like I'd just made the discovery of the century. My stomach started doing the same crazy dance it does when I wash a dill pickle down with orange juice.

I needed to think, but not here in the hall where Mr. Draper might see me. I needed privacy. So I tore into the girls' washroom across the hall. *Jeez!* The way I was panicking, you'd think *I* had done something wrong. I took a deep breath to calm down.

Okay. So what should I do?

The obvious option was to walk across the hall and tell Mr. Draper everything. Then the problem would be in his lap, and I could wash my hands of the whole thing. And lose my story, I reminded myself. Besides, if I told Draper everything, he would report it to the office. Then Mr. Wiens would know I'd lied to get students' marks.

Okay, forget that option.

What other choices did I have? I could always do nothing. I could walk away and let whatever was going to happen, happen. Yeah, right. Who was I kidding? I couldn't do that. I needed this story.

I sighed. It looked like I had only one real choice after all. I had to catch the crook in the act. But time was running out. If the thief was going to steal the answer key, it had to be soon.

I glanced at my watch. I didn't know how long I'd been in the washroom, but it must have been a while. It was way past four o'clock. Mr. Draper might even be gone.

I pulled the bathroom door open a crack. I didn't have much of a view— I could only see down the hall one way. But walking toward me—no, make that walking toward Mr. Draper's classroom—was Sean Leger.

I started to ease the door shut, but the sound of another door closing made me freeze. Sean stopped too.

"Sean," a jovial voice called. I figured it must be Mr. Draper. "What brings you this way?"

Sean shrugged and smiled— nervously, I thought. "Hi, Mr. Draper. I came to see if you needed me to do anything in the biology room?"

Mr. Draper came into my line of vision and put a hand on Sean's shoulder. "Thanks for asking, Sean, but I think we're good for a few days. There are some heavy labs next week, and I'm going to need a hand setting them up. Come back and see me then. In the meantime, you have a big math test to get ready for. I don't want to cut into your studying time." Then he chuckled. "You can walk me to my car and pick my brain about what's on it."

I watched them walk away. I was still staring through the crack in the door long after they'd disappeared down another hallway.

I was afraid to leave the washroom. I was afraid they'd come back. At least, I was afraid Sean would come back. When Mr. Draper had left his classroom, the only thing he was carrying was his coat. That meant he'd left the answer key in his office. It was the perfect time for Sean to steal it.

Chapter Ten

I stayed in the girls' bathroom another half hour, but Sean never returned, and I was getting tired of being trapped there. Bathrooms are okay places to do your business, but otherwise they're kind of gross. I'd already been in this one way too long.

It was getting late. Mom was probably wondering where I was. I dug around in my backpack for my phone, and with one eye on the hallway, I dialed home.

Jack answered.

"It's me," I said, hoping I sounded normal. I still felt tense from our run-in at lunch. "Is Mom there?"

"She's at the store. Where are you?" *He* sounded normal.

"At school," I replied. I prayed he wouldn't put two and two together.

No such luck. "What are you doing there?" he asked suspiciously. "School let out over an hour ago."

I heard a voice in the background. "Hey, man, get your sorry butt out here! Or are ya afraid I'm gonna kick it?"

"Hang on to your gitch, you wiener," Jack laughed.

"Who was that?"

"Leger." He laughed some more. "The guy's a moron. He thinks he's gonna beat me one on one."

I stopped breathing for a second. If Sean was playing basketball with Jack, he obviously wasn't coming back to the school.

Suddenly I couldn't get off the phone fast enough. "Well, anyway, I'm just leaving," I said in a rush. "Tell Mom I'm on my way." Before Jack could say anything else, I hung up.

Stuffing the phone back in my pack, I started for the exit. But after a couple of steps, I did a one-eighty and headed for the newspaper office instead. I needed to pick up the intro for my article so I could work on it over the weekend.

As I opened the door, I saw an envelope lying on the floor. I picked it up and turned it over. It was addressed to me. Was my informant sending me another clue?

The note inside was short and to the point. *If you don't stop snooping around, you're going to be sorry!* There was no signature. I flipped the paper over, but there was nothing more. I refolded the sheet and tapped it on my chin as I thought.

The threat was meant to scare me. The thing is, it didn't. It said I'd be sorry if I didn't stop snooping. Sorry about what? Sorry I stopped a thief? Hardly. Sorry kids were going to have to study for tests? Nope. I couldn't think of anything I might be sorry for—except maybe getting beat up or having my locker trashed. Somehow I couldn't imagine that happening.

Sean had written the note. I would have bet money on it. Jack probably told him about the article, and this was a big bluff to make me back off. But I wasn't falling for it. Sean might be dishonest, but he wasn't violent.

Of course, if someone else wrote the note, it could be a different story. Jack said a lot of kids at school were mad at me—everyone who was paying for cheat sheets, probably. How many did Liz say there were? An image of an angry mob chasing me through the halls filled my mind, and a shiver rippled down my spine.

Okay, so maybe I was a *little* scared, but not enough to stop, not when I was so close to getting my story.

If the crook didn't steal the answer key Monday, he wouldn't have another chance before the test. But if he did try to steal it, I was ready for him.

I hardly slept Sunday night. I kept imagining how things were going to unfold. I didn't think the scammer would strike at lunch hour. There were too many bodies roaming the school.

I holed up in the washroom across from Draper's math room at lunch anyway. Girls kept wandering in and out, so it was hard to keep a lookout. Not that it mattered. The thief never showed. I'd spent another hour in that disgusting hole for nothing.

By the time 3:30 rolled around, I was so antsy, I could have screamed. Every nerve in my body tingled.

As soon as the bell rang, I bolted for the washroom. I didn't even stop at my locker. The biology lab and math room were both empty. So was the glassed-in office between them.

For the first fifteen minutes, the washroom was busy with girls coming and going. I couldn't keep a close eye on Draper's room, but I wasn't worried. The thief wouldn't make his move until the traffic died down.

Around ten to four, things got quiet. I settled in at my post and got my phone ready to snap incriminating photos.

I didn't have to wait long. Within minutes, the crook showed up. He came from the other direction, so I didn't see him arrive. I only heard him. I wanted to open the door wider, but I didn't dare. I had to settle for listening. The sounds were the same as before—desk opening, keys jingling, filing cabinet drawer rolling open.

And then silence. What was happening? The suspense was killing me. I knew I was taking a big risk, but I had to find out. I stuck my head out the door and looked across the hall.

The thief was there—in the little glass office. He was rummaging through the filing cabinet. Finally he pulled out a paper—no, a Scantron sheet. It was the answer key, I was sure.

Instead of photographing it like I thought he would, he pulled a manila envelope out of his backpack and took another Scantron sheet out of it.

Even though I'd been imagining this moment for days, I couldn't believe what I was seeing. He was switching the sheets.

I didn't wait for him to finish. I couldn't. He might see me. I pulled my head back into the washroom, shut the door and waited for him to leave.

I looked down at the phone in my hand. I hadn't taken a single picture. I'd been too stunned. Jack had been right. Sean wasn't the thief.

Jack was.

Chapter Eleven

There had to be a mistake. My brother was *not* the Scantron Scammer. He couldn't be. Jack would *never* steal!

But he had. I'd seen him with my own eyes. He had broken into Mr. Draper's office and switched the answer keys. But why? He wasn't even in any of Draper's classes. And even if he was, Jack didn't need to cheat. He was a brain!

Had he done it for the money? That didn't make sense either. Our family wasn't rich, but we weren't poor. And Jack had a part-time job. He didn't need the money, unless—

Could my brother be doing drugs? I pushed the thought away before I finished thinking it. Jack was too into health and fitness to poison his body with chemicals. Besides, he wouldn't risk his basketball future.

I started to shake. Shock was setting in. The idea that Jack was a thief was almost more than I could stand. But he was still my brother! He might have done a bad thing, but he wasn't a bad person. I couldn't rat on him.

Then I heard something—not much, but enough to make me open the door a crack.

Someone was going into the room across the hall. Mr. Draper? The custodian? Maybe it was Jack again.

Maybe he'd had second thoughts and was returning the answer key.

I waited for the sound of the filing cabinet drawer rolling open. Then I poked my head out the door and looked toward the little office.

Someone was there. But it wasn't Jack. It wasn't Mr. Draper or the custodian either.

It was Sean.

He pulled the answer key out of its folder, placed it faceup on the desk, and took a photo of it with his phone. Then he slipped it inside the folder again and shut the filing cabinet.

I ducked back into the washroom, but kept my ear to the door. When I couldn't hear any more noises, I let myself into the hall.

Sean was gone.

Relief washed over me—for about three seconds.

What was going on? First my brother snuck into Draper's office and switched the answer keys. Then Sean broke in and photographed the one Jack left behind.

Were Jack and Sean *both* crooks? Did they know about each other? Were they part of the same scam?

I couldn't figure it out. If they were working together, why hadn't Sean taken a picture of the answer key *before* Jack made the switch? And why had Jack switched answer keys anyway? During the walk home, I kept trying to put the pieces of the puzzle together, but nothing seemed to fit.

As I turned onto my street, I slowed down, which was really stupid, considering it was pouring rain. I hardly noticed. I was more worried about facing my brother than I was about getting soaked.

What was I going to do? Was I going to tell him that I'd seen him in Mr. Draper's classroom? Was I going to demand an explanation? Would I threaten to turn him in? What if he refused to confess, even when I confronted him with the facts?

I had no idea what I was going to do. Maybe nothing—at least not right away. I needed time to think. I'd seen Jack in Draper's office, but he hadn't seen me. He had no idea I was on to him. If I could hide my feelings, he wouldn't suspect a thing. I'm not very good at stifling my emotions, so it would take a miracle to pull that one off. My best bet was to avoid Jack altogether.

I didn't get the chance. He was waiting for me in the upstairs hallway. He was slouched in the doorway to his bedroom, and he looked like he'd aged ten years since I'd last seen him.

"I need to talk to you," he said.

"About what?" I mumbled, avoiding his gaze.

He pushed himself away from the wall and walked into his room. "I think you know."

Chapter Twelve

My brain screamed *No!*

I wasn't ready to face Jack. But my body followed him anyway.

I hadn't even closed the door before he started in on me.

"I'm going to ask you one more time, Laurel. Don't write this article. I asked you before—for Sean. Now I'm asking you for me."

Suddenly I was laughing. But it wasn't a *boy-did-that-ever-tickle-my-funny-bone* laugh. It was the kind of laugh you would expect to roll out of a person who was about to become an ax murderer. I was definitely losing it. The look on Jack's face confirmed it.

He frowned and—yes—he actually took a step backward. "What's the matter with you?"

That brought me back to my senses. "What's the matter with *me*?" I repeated in amazement. "The more accurate question is, what's the matter with *you*?"

"What are you talking about? I'm not the one cackling my head off like a crazy person."

"And I'm not the one up to my eyebrows in a cheating scam!" I shot back.

There. I'd said it. The color drained from Jack's face. I could tell my words had hit home. I wished I could take them back.

"I saw you in Draper's office today," I said. It wasn't an accusation—just a fact. "I saw you switch the answer keys."

I wanted him to deny it, but he just slumped onto the bed and stared at the rug. "It's complicated."

I didn't say anything.

He reached over to his desk and picked up a large brown envelope. No doubt it was the one he'd had in Mr. Draper's office. He placed it on the bed beside him.

Then he looked at me. "All I ask is that you hear me out. After that, you can do whatever you want."

I nodded.

"Okay," he said. "You were right about Sean. He is selling cheat sheets. But it didn't start out that way," he added. "Sean's a good guy, but he's not a great student, especially not in math. Believe me, I know what I'm talking about. I've studied with him. For Sean, math is a foreign language. He just doesn't get it."

"That doesn't make it okay for him to cheat."

Jack scowled at me. "You said you'd listen."

"Sorry."

"At the beginning of the school year, Sean got on as Mr. Draper's biology assistant. I think he was hoping it would give him an edge with his assignments. It also gave him a bit of spending money, which Sean doesn't have a lot of. Cash is pretty tight around his house.

"The first time he cheated was at the start of basketball season. There was a big math test, and Sean had to pass it or he'd get booted off the team. He found the answer key by accident when Mr. Draper sent him to get something. And"—Jack shrugged—"the temptation was too much. He photographed it. Then he made himself a cheat sheet with just enough right answers to make it look like a legitimate pass."

"So how did it turn into a business?"

"I'm getting to that." Jack cleared his throat and settled back into his story. "I didn't know about the cheating until the second time. We had a big tournament coming up, and Sean didn't have the money to go. That's when he came up with the idea to sell cheat sheets. He had practically a whole class of customers in no time. He knew he couldn't give everyone the actual answer key. If the whole class aced a test, he'd get caught for sure. But he had no idea how to figure out how many right answers each kid needed to end up with their usual mark."

"That's where you came in."

Jack sighed. "When Sean first asked me to help, I freaked out and told him no way. But he said he'd already used the money to pay for the basketball trip. If he didn't come up with the cheat sheets, he'd be toast. The kids in his class would either rat on him or kill him."

Jack's eyes pleaded with me to understand. "Sean's my friend. I had to help him."

"But it happened again."

He nodded.

"How many times?"

"One time after that, and then I told Sean I was done. No more. Basketball season was pretty much over, so there was no reason for him to cheat anymore."

"But—"

"But he didn't want to quit. He's been hounding me to help him one last time. But I told him flat out—no. So he said he'd do it on his own."

Jack looked miserable.

"So you gave in."

His head shot up. "No! I already feel like crud for helping him as much as I have. I won't do it again. I *can't* do it again." He paused before adding, "And I can't let *him* do it either."

He picked up the envelope and opened it.

"When you saw me today in Draper's office, I was switching the real answer key for a fake. If Sean tries to sell cheat sheets using that, everyone is going to fail, and he'll be as good as dead."

"So now what?"

"So now I call him and tell him he's got the wrong answers." He flopped back onto the bed and stared at the ceiling. "He is going to be so pissed off."

"Maybe," I conceded, "but at least he won't get in trouble."

Chapter Thirteen

The cheating scam was supposed to be my ticket to fame. It was a juicy scandal I could take to the editor of the *Islander*. With a reputation as an ace reporter, I would finally be recognized for me and not just as Jack Quinn's little sister.

All I cared about was the glory my article was going to win me. Jack was right about that. As long as the scammer was some faceless kid in school, everything was fine. I didn't think about what would happen after I exposed him. I was even okay with the situation when I thought Sean was involved.

But when I found out Jack was part of the scam too, things weren't so black and white anymore. Jack had done a bad thing, but he wasn't a bad person. And there was no way I was going to tell everyone at school—*everyone in the city!*—what he'd done. But to reveal only Sean's part wouldn't be fair either.

So my story was dead.

I still had to write an article though. So I wrote about me. Well, sort of. I wrote about the things I'd learned while chasing the story.

I wrote about how everyone hated me after the first article on cheating. I said I thought I had a responsibility to report the story. But maybe all those kids who were mad at me had a point. I'd only been seeing the facts, not the people. I said that Jarod and Dale may have cheated—I still didn't mention their names— but instead of seeing what they did as a crime, I now saw it as an act of friendship.

I wrote how there is always more than one side to a story, and I apologized for judging others. Sometimes the reasons people do things are just as important as the things they do. And most important, I told my readers—if there were any left—that at the end of the day, we have to be able to live with ourselves. It wasn't the article I'd planned to write. It was the one I needed to write. I worked on it for days.

It didn't erase the harm I'd done. It didn't make kids start talking to me again, but I knew I had learned from my mistakes, and that was a start.

The morning after the paper came out, there was another envelope waiting for me in the newspaper office.

As soon as I started to read it, I knew it was from my informant. It said, *I gave you the story on a platter, but you jammed out. You blew it.*

Great! Now my informant hated me too. Most people were mad at me for the stuff I'd written. This guy—I assumed it was a guy from the handwriting—was mad at me for what I *hadn't* written.

After morning announcements, Sean got hauled into the principal's office. Apparently my informant had taken matters into his own hands. Since I wasn't going to write about the scam, he had decided to go to Mr. Wiens himself. But he didn't know about Jack's involvement.

Even though Sean was still mad at Jack, he never ratted him out. Sean could have denied his own part in the scam too—it was his word against another student's—but he confessed everything.

Sean got kicked out of Barton High and was transferred to another school. That meant he wasn't going to graduate with the kids he'd known since kindergarten.

What Sean had done was wrong, but it's not like he was headed for a life of crime. He'd just had a weak moment. If I hadn't put out that survey, no one would ever have found out. On the other hand, my informant might have gone to the principal anyway. There was no way of knowing, but I still felt like the situation was my fault.

My conscience was bugging me, but it was nothing compared to what Jack was going through. I stopped by his room the day Sean got kicked out to see how he was doing.

"It's my fault!" he groaned as he paced his room. "If I'd stuck to my guns the first time, the whole thing would've died right then."

"You've got a very convenient memory, Jack," I said drily. "Sean had spent the money before he even handed over the cheat sheets. Remember? If you hadn't helped him, he would've got the crap beat out of him. Would that have made you feel better?"

He sent me a withering glare and continued to pace. "Well, I should've done something," he muttered. "Pay back the money maybe."

"Since when do *you* have that kind of cash?" I hooted. "Sean made six hundred dollars for one math test!"

"I could've—"

"Give it a rest, Jack," I interrupted him. "This isn't your fault. Sean knows that. Which is why he didn't take you down with him."

Jack sank onto the bed. "It's not right that he's taking the fall for this alone."

"What possible good would it do for you to be in trouble too? It wouldn't change anything for Sean."

"I know," he said. "But it might change things for me. You said it yourself, Laurel. At the end of the day, we all have to be able to live with ourselves."

Jack confessed to Mom and Dad, and the next morning he told the whole story to Mr. Wiens.

He was stretched out on his bed, staring at the ceiling when I knocked on his door after school.

"So what happened?" I asked after he gave me the okay to come in.

"I'm suspended." He didn't sound angry or even upset. It was just a statement of fact.

"For how long?"

"Two weeks. Mom and Dad also grounded me."

"Is that all?" I asked.

Jack lifted his head and squinted at me. "Isn't that enough?"

"What I mean is, did you get transferred to another school too—like Sean?"

He sat up and swung his legs over the edge of the bed. "No. But Mr. Wiens made it crystal clear that if basketball wasn't finished for the year, I'd be off the team."

"Oh," I said. "Well, that's sort of lucky then. You couldn't have been scouted by all those colleges if that had happened."

"Yeah, well maybe that would have been just as well. Then I wouldn't have gotten my hopes up."

"What do you mean?" I asked warily.

He smiled, but it was pretty pathetic. "Do you remember how Mr. Wiens and my coach sent out letters of recommendation to all the colleges that were recruiting me?"

I nodded. "Yeah. So?"

"Well, Mr. Wiens says that now he is obligated to let all those schools know what I did."

"Oh no," I gasped. "Does that mean they'll take back their scholarship offers?"

Jack shrugged. "I don't know. Mr. Wiens said he doesn't view what I did as a morality issue so much as a lapse in judgment, and that's how he plans to present it in his letter."

"That's good—right?" I asked hopefully.

"I don't know." He shrugged again. "I guess we'll have to wait and see."

I nodded. I felt empty—flat. Everything had gone so wrong. The big article that was supposed to put me on the social map had done exactly the opposite. It had turned me into an outcast, ruined Sean's and Jack's reputations, strained their friendship and maybe even cost Jack his basketball future.

Yeah, things had backfired all right. All I could do now was hope they'd improve. But like Jack said—we'd have to wait and see.

Kristin Butcher is the author of numerous popular books for juveniles, including *Chat Room* in the Orca Currents series. She has never cheated on a test. Kristin lives in Campbell River, British Columbia.

orca *currents*

The following is an excerpt from
another exciting Orca Currents novel,
Chat Room by Kristin Butcher.

978-1-55143-485-8 $9.95 pb

When Linda's high school sets up
online chat rooms, she can't resist the urge to
visit them. Fueled by interest in a student with the
nickname Cyrano, Linda participates in online
conversations using the nickname Roxanne and
gains a reputation as the queen of one-liners. Soon
Linda starts receiving gifts from a secret admirer
who signs his gifts "C." She is certain that her life
has taken a turn for the better until "C" reveals his
true identity.

Chapter One

Back in elementary school, assemblies meant sitting on the floor. In high school things are different. Because we're older now, we sit in actual chairs—at least that's the theory. If you're one of the first people into the gym, the system works fine. But I always arrive after every seat's been taken. If there's not a person sitting in it, it's being saved for someone. Basically, it's a school-wide version of musical chairs, and I've always sucked at that game.

Take Friday's assembly. The gym was packed as usual, but for once it looked like I was going to get lucky. There was an empty seat at the end of the third row. I would have preferred something a little farther back, but it was that or nothing. So I grabbed it.

Unfortunately Janice saw me and started waving from the middle of the row. I wanted to pretend I didn't see her, but I knew if I did she'd unleash that bullhorn voice of hers, and in two seconds I'd have every kid in school staring at me. So I bumped my way through the line of knees separating us and shriveled into the seat beside her.

"What class are you missing?" Whispering wasn't a skill Janice had ever learned, and, even though everyone around us was talking, her voice drowned them out.

"Math," I said, shrinking a little deeper into my chair. I intentionally avoided asking her what she was missing, but that didn't stop Janice.

"It's biology for me. *Thank God*! If I had to miss band I'd be ticked, but I can definitely do without forty minutes of Bio-Bernstein droning on about reproduction. What have they dragged us in here for anyway?"

I shrugged. "I don't know. The gym riot maybe? There are posters about it up all over school." I nodded toward a group of students huddled around the microphone. "It looks like student council's running the assembly, so I bet that's what it is."

Janice rolled her eyes and flopped back in her chair. "Oh, joy! Just what we need—another chance for Wellington High's favored few to show off."

I wasn't sure if Janice was referring to the gym riot or student council running the assembly. Probably both. She was against everything social.

Janice Beastly was queen of the grumps. Her real name was *Beasley*, but she was so negative and in-your-face that everybody called her Beastly. It didn't help that she was built like a wrestler with a voice to match. She didn't have a lot of friends. None, actually, unless you counted me.

Even that was only friendship by default. I didn't like Janice any more than anyone else did, but when she showed up at the start of grade nine, she adopted me. And since her locker was right beside mine, I was stuck.

Maybe I should have been grateful, because except for Janice, I don't have many friends either. Not that people hate me. At least I don't think they do. I'm just not part of any crowd.

The microphone squealed.

"Sorry about that," said the boy standing in front of it. It was Marc Solomon, student council president and one of the most popular guys in school. He grinned. "But now that I have your attention, let's get this party started. The first thing on today's agenda is the big gym riot coming up next Friday."

Behind him the student council started clapping and cheering, and in a matter of seconds the audience joined in.

Marc leaned into the mic. "That's the spirit, Wellington!"

"Oh, spare me," Janice muttered.

Marc held up his hands for quiet. "As always, the riot's going to be a blast, and this year we've added a whole bunch of new events like tricycle basketball, egg toss and a chain-gang relay."

"What's that?" someone hollered.

Marc grinned again. "I'll get to that. That and all the other details."

He turned and gestured toward a pretty blond girl standing behind him. She smiled and waved. "Thanks to our student council vice-president, the teachers have agreed to give us gym riot planning time," he paused, "last period this afternoon."

"Hey, that's my band class!" Janice protested, but her complaint was lost in the roar that erupted around us.

When it got quiet again, Marc motioned for a boy in the front row to join him at the microphone. Hesitantly, the kid stood up. It was Chad Sharp. I recognized him from French class.

"Right now, though, I want to tell you about a totally new and exciting feature that's just been added to the school's website." Marc clapped Chad on the back. "And this guy here is the mastermind behind it. For those of you who don't know him, let me introduce Chad Sharp."

There was a bit of applause, and Chad's cheeks went red. I felt sorry for him. If I had to stand up in front of a thousand kids, I'd probably die.

Marc gestured for Chad to take over the mic, but Chad shook his head.

"A man of big ideas, but few words," Marc said, resuming his spot in front of the microphone. "But that's okay. The important thing is that thanks to Chad and the parent council, we now have a chat room on our school website."

An instant buzz spread through the gym.

"You heard right." Marc nodded. "A chat room. Actually, it's lots of chat rooms. There's something for everybody. If you want to compare notes about movies or music or the newest fads, you can visit *The Hot Spot*. For you athletic types, there's a sports chat room. Want to talk about the stuff going on at school? Go to the

Wellington Room. If you just need to let off steam, there's a chat room for that too. There's even a *Homework Help* chat room."

Excited pockets of chatter sprang up around the gym, and it took Marc a good minute to get everyone quiet again.

"There will be some rules, of course," he said. "This could be a really good thing, so we don't want anybody messing it up."

"What kind of rules?" someone asked.

"Well, for starters, only Wellington students will have access. Secondly, when you enter a chat room you have to use a nickname. And thirdly, you can't gross out or talk about other students."

A hand went up. "If your identity is secret, how will anyone know if you're breaking the rules?"

"Good question," Marc said. "The office will monitor the chat rooms.

When you log on, you'll exchange your student number and e-mail address for a nickname. No one will have access to your personal information except the site administrator—a.k.a. Mr. Barnes in computer science. To everyone online, you'll be anonymous. But if you break the rules, the office will track you down and you'll be toast. Any other questions?"

Hands shot up all over the place.

"This is the stupidest thing I've ever heard," Janice grumbled, making it impossible for me to hear the questions and answers. Even a glare from the girl in front of Janice didn't shut her up. "I can't believe the principal is going along with this lame idea. Chat rooms are nothing but hangouts for perverts. Anybody who visits them is asking for trouble."

Titles in the Series

orca currents